JUL 1 2 2019

D1105603

Perritano, John

362.29
PER

Performance-
enhancing drugs

HUDSON PUBLIC LIBRARY
3 WASHINGTON STREET
HUDSON, MA 01749
ADULT: 978-568-9644
CHILDREN: 978-568-9645
www.hudsonpubliclibrary.com

Performance-Enhancing Drugs:
Steroids, Hormones, and Supplements

Performance-Enhancing Drugs:
Steroids, Hormones, and Supplements

John Perritano

SERIES CONSULTANT
SARA BECKER, Ph.D.
Brown University School of Public Health
Warren Alpert Medical School

MASON CREST

Mason Crest
450 Parkway Drive, Suite D
Broomall, PA 19008
www.masoncrest.com

© 2017 by Mason Crest, an imprint of National Highlights, Inc. All rights reserved.
No part of this publication may be reproduced or transmitted in any form or by any
means, electronic or mechanical, including photocopying, recording, taping, or
any information storage and retrieval system, without permission from the publisher.

MTM Publishing, Inc.
www.mtmpublishing.com

President: Valerie Tomaselli
Vice President, Book Development: Hilary Poole
Designer: Annemarie Redmond
Copyeditor: Peter Jaskowiak
Editorial Assistant: Andrea St. Aubin

Series ISBN: 978-1-4222-3598-0
Hardback ISBN: 978-1-4222-3609-3
E-Book ISBN: 978-1-4222-8253-3

Library of Congress Cataloging-in-Publication Data
Names: Perritano, John, author.
Title: Performance-enhancing drugs : steroids, hormones, and supplements / by
    John Perritano.
Description: Mason Crest : Broomall, PA, [2017] | Series: Drug addiction and
    recovery | Includes bibliiographical references and index.
Identifiers: LCCN 2016003955| ISBN 9781422236093 (hardback) | ISBN
    9781422235980 (series) | ISBN 9781422282533 (ebook)
Subjects: LCSH: Doping in sports—Juvenile literature. | Athletes—Drug use—Juvenile
    literature. | Anabolic steroids—Health aspects—Juvenile literature. | Hormones—
    Physiological effect—Juvenile literature. | Somatotropin—Health aspects—Juvenile
    literature.
Classification: LCC RC1230 .P4784 2017 | DDC 362.29/088/796—dc23
LC record available at http://lccn.loc.gov/2016003955

Printed and bound in the United States of America.

First printing
9 8 7 6 5 4 3 2 1

QR CODES AND LINKS TO THIRD PARTY CONTENT
You may gain access to certain third party content ("Third Party Sites") by scanning and using
the QR Codes that appear in this publication (the "QR Codes"). We do not operate or control in
any respect any information, products or services on such Third Party Sites linked to by us via
the QR Codes included in this publication and we assume no responsibility for any materials you
may access using the QR Codes. Your use of the QR Codes may be subject to terms, limitations,
or restrictions set forth in the applicable terms of use or otherwise established by the owners
of the Third Party Sites. Our linking to such Third Party Sites via the QR Codes does not imply an
endorsement or sponsorship of such Third Party Sites, or the information, products or services
offered on or through the Third Party Sites, nor does it imply an endorsement or sponsorship of this
publication by the owners of such Third Party Sites.

TABLE OF CONTENTS

Key Icons to Look for:

Words to Understand: These words with their easy-to-understand definitions will increase the reader's understanding of the text, while building vocabulary skills.

Sidebars: This boxed material within the main text allows readers to build knowledge, gain insights, explore possibilities, and broaden their perspectives by weaving together additional information to provide realistic and holistic perspectives.

Research Projects: Readers are pointed toward areas of further inquiry connected to each chapter. Suggestions are provided for projects that encourage deeper research and analysis.

Text-Dependent Questions: These questions send the reader back to the text for more careful attention to the evidence presented there.

Educational Videos: Readers can view videos by scanning our QR codes, providing them with additional educational content to supplement the text. Examples include news coverage, moments in history, speeches, iconic sports moments and much more!

Series Glossary of Key Terms: This back-of-the-book glossary contains terminology used throughout the series. Words found here increase the reader's ability to read and comprehend higher-level books and articles in this field.

SERIES INTRODUCTION

Many adolescents in the United States will experiment with alcohol or other drugs by time they finish high school. According to a 2014 study funded by the National Institute on Drug Abuse, about 27 percent of 8th graders have tried alcohol, 20 percent have tried drugs, and 13 percent have tried cigarettes. By 12th grade, these rates more than double: 66 percent of 12th graders have tried alcohol, 50 percent have tried drugs, and 35 percent have tried cigarettes.

Adolescents who use substances experience an increased risk of a wide range of negative consequences, including physical injury, family conflict, school truancy, legal problems, and sexually transmitted diseases. Higher rates of substance use are also associated with the leading causes of death in this age group: accidents, suicide, and violent crime. Relative to adults, adolescents who experiment with alcohol or other drugs progress more quickly to a full-blown substance use disorder and have more co-occurring mental health problems.

The National Survey on Drug Use and Health (NSDUH) estimated that in 2015 about 1.3 million adolescents between the ages of 12 and 17 (5 percent of adolescents in the United States) met the medical criteria for a substance use disorder. Unfortunately, the vast majority of these

IF YOU NEED HELP NOW . . .

SAMHSA's National Helpline provides referrals for mental-health or substance-use counseling.
1-800-662-HELP (4357) or https://findtreatment.samhsa.gov

SAMHSA's National Suicide Prevention Lifeline provides crisis counseling by phone or online, 24-hours-a-day and 7 days a week.
1-800-273-TALK (8255) or http://www.suicidepreventionlifeline.org

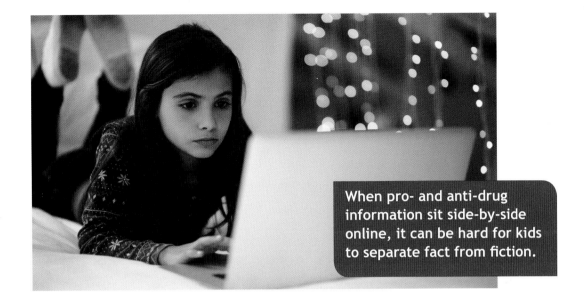

When pro- and anti-drug information sit side-by-side online, it can be hard for kids to separate fact from fiction.

adolescents did not receive treatment. Less than 10 percent of those with a diagnosis received specialty care, leaving 1.2 million adolescents with an unmet need for treatment.

The NSDUH asked the 1.2 million adolescents with untreated substance use disorders why they didn't receive specialty care. Over 95 percent said that they didn't think they needed it. The other 5 percent reported challenges finding quality treatment that was covered by their insurance. Very few treatment providers and agencies offer substance use treatment designed to meet the specific needs of adolescents. Meanwhile, numerous insurance plans have "opted out" of providing coverage for addiction treatment, while others have placed restrictions on what is covered.

Stigma about substance use is another serious problem. We don't call a person with an eating disorder a "food abuser," but we use terms like "drug abuser" to describe individuals with substance use disorders. Even treatment providers often unintentionally use judgmental words, such as describing urine screen results as either "clean" or "dirty." Underlying this language is the idea that a substance use disorder is some kind of moral failing or character flaw, and that people with these disorders deserve blame or punishment for their struggles.

And punish we do. A 2010 report by CASA Columbia found that in the United States, 65 percent of the 2.3 million people in prisons and jails met medical criteria for a substance use disorder, while another 20 percent had histories of substance use disorders, committed their crimes while under the influence of alcohol or drugs, or committed a substance-related crime. Many of these inmates spend decades in prison, but only 11 percent of them receive any treatment during their incarceration. Our society invests significantly more money in punishing individuals with substance use disorders than we do in treating them.

At a basic level, the ways our society approaches drugs and alcohol—declaring a "war on drugs," for example, or telling kids to "Just Say No!"—reflect a misunderstanding about the nature of addiction. The reality is that addiction is a disease that affects all types of people—parents and children, rich and poor, young and old. Substance use disorders stem from a complex interplay of genes, biology, and the environment, much like most physical and mental illnesses.

The way we talk about recovery, using phrases like "kick the habit" or "breaking free," also misses the mark. Substance use disorders are chronic, insidious, and debilitating illnesses. Fortunately, there are a number of effective treatments for substance use disorders. For many patients, however, the road is long and hard. Individuals recovering from substance use disorders can experience horrible withdrawal symptoms, and many will continue to struggle with cravings for alcohol or drugs. It can be a daily struggle to cope with these cravings and stay abstinent. A popular saying at Alcoholics Anonymous (AA) meetings is "one day at a time," because every day of recovery should be respected and celebrated.

There are a lot of incorrect stereotypes about individuals with substance use disorders, and there is a lot of false information about the substances, too. If you do an Internet search on the term "marijuana," for instance, two top hits are a web page by the National Institute on Drug Abuse and a page operated by Weedmaps, a medical and recreational marijuana dispensary. One of these pages publishes scientific information and one publishes pro-marijuana articles. Both pages have a high-quality, professional appearance. If you had never heard of either organization, it would be hard to know which to trust. It can be really difficult for the average person, much less the average teenager, to navigate these waters.

The topics covered in this series were specifically selected to be relevant to teenagers. About half of the volumes cover the types of drugs that they are most likely to hear about or to come in contact with. The other half cover important issues related to alcohol and other drug use (which we refer to as "drug use" in the titles for simplicity). These books cover topics such as the causes of drug use, the influence of drug use on the family, drug use and the legal system, drug use and mental health, and treatment options. Many teens will either have personal experience with these issues or will know someone who does.

This series was written to help young people get the facts about common drugs, substance use disorders, substance-related problems, and recovery. Accurate information can help adolescents to make better decisions. Students who are educated can help each other to better understand the risks and consequences of drug use. Facts also go a long way to reducing the stigma associated with substance use. We tend to fear or avoid things that we don't understand. Knowing the facts can make it easier to support each other. For students who know someone struggling with a substance use disorder, these books can also help them know what to expect. If they are worried about someone, or even about themselves, these books can help to provide some answers and a place to start.

—Sara J. Becker, Ph.D., Assistant Professor (Research), Center for Alcohol and Addictions Studies, Brown University School of Public Health, Assistant Professor (Research), Department of Psychiatry and Human Behavior, Brown University Medical School

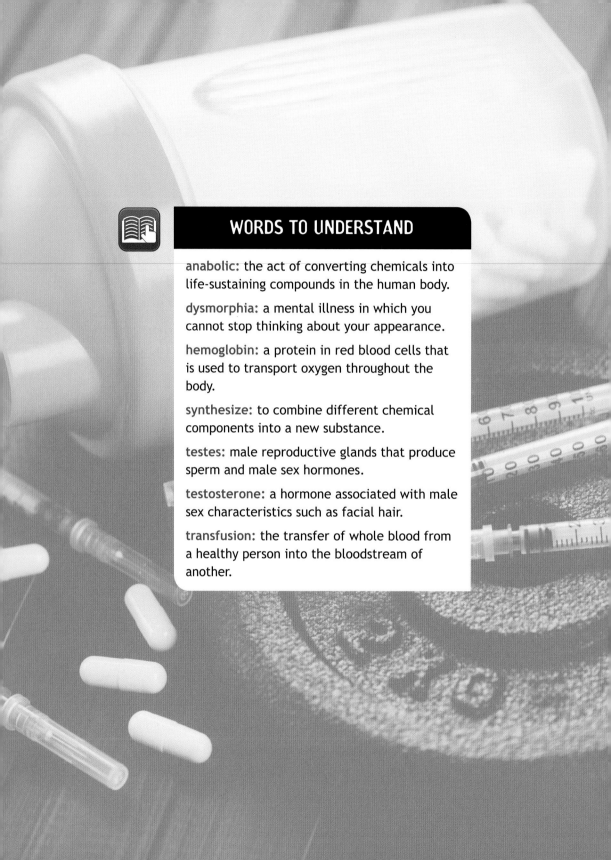

WORDS TO UNDERSTAND

anabolic: the act of converting chemicals into life-sustaining compounds in the human body.

dysmorphia: a mental illness in which you cannot stop thinking about your appearance.

hemoglobin: a protein in red blood cells that is used to transport oxygen throughout the body.

synthesize: to combine different chemical components into a new substance.

testes: male reproductive glands that produce sperm and male sex hormones.

testosterone: a hormone associated with male sex characteristics such as facial hair.

transfusion: the transfer of whole blood from a healthy person into the bloodstream of another.

CHAPTER ONE

WHAT ARE PERFORMANCE-ENHANCING DRUGS?

Perhaps no sporting event is as grueling and as body-punishing as the Tour de France, the world's premier cycling event. The 21-stage race covers some 2,089 miles (3,360 km)—about the distance from Chicago to San Francisco—and includes treacherous mountain climbs across the Pyrenees Mountains in France and along the French Alps. Four cyclists have won the Tour five times. Only the American Lance Armstrong has won the race seven consecutive times, which he did from 1999 to 2005. It was a remarkable feat of endurance for anyone, but especially for Armstrong, who had overcome a life-and-death struggle with cancer.

Lance Armstrong riding in the Tour de France.

There was one problem with Armstrong's accomplishments—he cheated. Armstrong was injecting himself with performance-enhancing drugs, or PEDs. In 2013, Armstrong admitted taking the male sex hormone testosterone and human growth hormone (HGH) to boost his performance. He also admitted using EPO, or erythropoietin, a hormone that increases the amount of oxygen flowing to a person's muscles. EPO is supposed to give endurance athletes like Armstrong a competitive boost. In addition to taking these banned substances, Armstrong also admitted he had used oxygen-boosting blood transfusions.

Many people had suspected that Armstrong was using PEDs. Their suspicious were confirmed by a report by the United States Anti-Doping Agency (USADA), which tests American athletes for PEDs. Armstrong, once the Superman of cycling, was stripped of his seven Tour de France victories and the Olympic bronze medal he had won at the 2000 Summer Olympic Games. He was also kicked out of cycling, becoming a pariah in the sport he once dominated. Armstrong's dramatic fall came after years of steadfastly denying he used PEDs.

Not only did Armstrong lose his medals, championships, and awards, but he also lost his reputation. Sadly, Armstrong is not alone. Thousands of professional and amateur athletes, including teenagers, use illegal steroids or other PEDs. It's a win-at-no-cost attitude that can have dire consequences. Despite the laurels and awards, Armstrong put himself at great risk. Long-term use of PEDs can create myriad physical and psychological problems that could end in death.

THE DESIRE TO WIN

Athletes take PEDs in the hopes of gaining a competitive edge. The drugs allow athletes to train harder and longer. As a result, they become faster and stronger. However, PEDs are banned by professional sports organizations for a number of reasons. First, they give athletes an unfair advantage. Second, they are dangerous: the drugs can wreak havoc on users' bodies and even alter how their brains work. PED users can suffer a range of lifelong problems, including infertility, heart and liver damage, difficulty managing aggression, and depression. Some have committed suicide or harmed others.

However, the risks of stiff penalties for PED use in some sports have done little to curb their use. In fact, despite Armstrong's PED legacy, PED use—also called "juicing"—is still widespread in cycling and many other sports.

The constant refrain sports fans hear from athletes is that PEDs "level the playing field." In other words, because their opponents are juicing, they have no choice but to take PEDs, too. To see this phenomenon in action, one only has to look at the 1998 Major League Baseball season, in which Mark McGwire of the St. Louis Cardinals and Sammy Sosa of the Chicago Cubs chased Roger Maris's 37-year-old single-season home run record. McGwire slugged 70 homers that season, breaking Maris' record by nine homers. The following year, Barry Bonds of the San Francisco Giants hit 73, besting McGwire's total. But it wasn't long before Sosa, McGwire, Bonds, and other top stars in baseball soon became mixed up in the greatest PED scandal in sports history. Baseball officials later conducted an inquiry into PED use, revealing that 5 percent of the 1,438 major-league players in the early 2000s had tested positive for PEDs.

McGwire (who later admitted using PEDs) and Bonds (who has never admitted using them), along with other top stars, including the pitcher Roger Clemens, have been denied induction into the Baseball Hall of Fame, the highest honor in the game, due to suspicions of PED use.

In addition to the physical and mental consequences, PED users take the drugs in the shadows, jeopardizing their careers, their lives, and their reputations. Yet the allure of these drugs is so powerful that many athletes have had a hard time acknowledging the negative consequences of their actions.

There are a few different ways to take PEDs; one is via injection.

"I don't recommend steroids for everyone, and I don't recommend growth hormones for everyone," said the former baseball star Jose Canseco, who used PEDs during his carrier. "But for certain individuals, I truly believe, because I've experimented with it for so many years, that it can make an average athlete a super athlete. It can make a super athlete incredible. Just legendary."

MAGIC SUBSTANCES?

When people use the term "performance-enhancing drugs," they are specifically talking about any drug that athletes take to improve performance. These drugs include **anabolic** steroids, HGH, stimulants, and diuretics, which help the body expel unneeded water through urination.

WHAT IS BLOOD DOPING?

Blood doping is a method of artificially boosting the amount of oxygen in the bloodstream. Blood doping can be done in two ways. The first is when athletes give themselves their own blood through transfusions. They remove and then store their blood weeks before a competition, and then they inject the stored blood back into their bodies prior to game time. By that time, the body has replaced the blood initially taken out. The extra blood increases the levels of hemoglobin, an oxygen-carrying protein, in their bloodstream.

The second method is for an athlete to inject themselves with EPO or other substances that increase the amount of oxygen in the blood. In each case, the body has more oxygenated blood than normal. The body's muscles drink up the oxygen-soaked blood, allowing athletes to run faster and farther, and also train harder.

Blood doping is a dangerous technique. It increases the number of red blood cells, which in effect thickens the blood. As a result, the heart has to work faster than it usually does to pump blood throughout the body. For this reason, blood doping raises the risk of heart attacks, blood clots, and strokes.

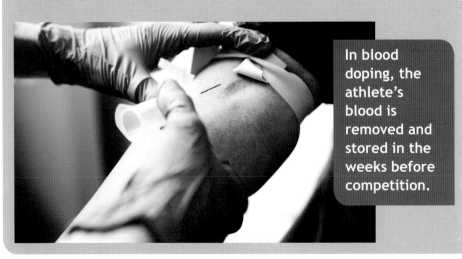

In blood doping, the athlete's blood is removed and stored in the weeks before competition.

Using performance-enhancing substances is nothing new in sports. Athletes in ancient Greece drank a juice made of mushrooms and herbs that they hoped would make them stronger. The Romans choked back a special herbal brew before competing at the Circus Maximus, which was essentially an ancient Daytona 500, in which men raced chariots around a circular track.

Yet, it wasn't until the mid-20th century that the modern era of performance enhancing drugs emerged. At the 1952 Summer Olympics in Helsinki, Finland, weightlifters from the Soviet Union dominated the games. They won seven medals in seven different

The Discobolus of Myron depicts an athlete from Ancient Greece, around 460-450 BCE.

events. More than a few heads turned at the Soviet success, including the head of U.S. weightlifting coach Bob Hoffman. Hoffman suspected the Soviets were taking drugs to increase their strength. His suspicions were confirmed two years later when John Ziegler, the U.S. weightlifting team physician, learned from the Soviet team doctor that the Soviet athletes were using testosterone to build muscle. Doctors injected the athletes with the hormone, which jump-started the body's ability to gain strength.

Ziegler returned to the United States and gave it a try himself. He experimented on a group of weightlifters at a gym in York, Pennsylvania. Ziegler, however, wasn't happy with the results. The York weightlifters didn't gain much strength or muscle mass. Many complained of feeling sick or hurt. Undaunted, Ziegler continued his research and continued to experiment. In 1958, Ciba Pharmaceuticals began selling his creation, Dianabol. The drug was a **synthesized** version of testosterone called methandrostenolone.

Ziegler gave the York weightlifters Dianabol. They trained harder and became beefier and stronger. Other weightlifters took note. They saw how well the drug was working and used "Doc Ziegler's mysterious pink pills"

Weightlifting is one sport where extra strength can give competitors an edge.

PED USE IN SPORTS

1886: Cyclist Arthur Linton from Wales dies during a race in France. He apparently consumed a toxic mix of alcohol, strychnine (a poison), heroin, caffeine, and cocaine to gain an edge.

1904: Thomas Hicks wins an Olympic gold medal in the marathon after taking strychnine and drinking down raw eggs and brandy during the race.

1954: Dr. John Ziegler begins experimenting with testosterone injections. A year later, Ciba Pharmaceuticals starts selling Dianabol, an anabolic steroid.

1975: The International Olympic Committee bans anabolic steroids.

1988: Olympic sprinter Ben Johnson is stripped of his gold medal when he tests positive for PEDs.

1992: NFL star Lyle Alzado dies of brain cancer. He had admitted using PEDs over a 20-year period.

1999: The World Anti-Doping Agency is formed by the International Olympic Committee.

2004: Evidence reveals that between 500 and 2,000 East German athletes suffer from various diseases, including cancer, because of their use of steroids years earlier.

2007: Major League Baseball publishes a report into the illegal use of PEDs by professional baseball players.

2013: Cyclist Lance Armstrong admits using PEDs. He is stripped of an Olympic medal and seven Tour de France wins.

themselves. However, most did not follow Ziegler's instructions regarding how much of the drug to take. Those seeking more of a competitive edge took high doses of the drug. And when Ziegler examined the bodybuilders, he found that several had problems with their genitals, including enlarged prostate glands and shrunken **testes**. Ziegler eventually spoke out against his wonder pills. "It is bad enough to have to deal with drug addicts, but now healthy athletes are putting themselves in the same category," he later wrote. "It's a disgrace. Who plays sports for fun anymore?"

But by then, the PED genie was out of the bottle. By 1968 the World Health Organization officially complained that drug companies were overproducing steroids. In the 1970s, PEDs became so widespread in sports that the International Olympic Committee banned their use. Since then, all professional sports, including Major League Baseball, the National Football League, and the National Basketball Association have banned their use. The NBA, for example, began drug testing in 1983. It has banned 100 substances. Yet, some PEDs are difficult to detect. The NFL began testing its athletes in 1987, and has continued to add drugs to the banned list. In 2014, it began testing blood to detect HGH.

TEENS AND PEDS

Adult athletes are not the only people using PEDs. Over the past several years, an increasing number of teens have used the drugs. In 2015 the Partnership for Drug-Free Kids reported that 11 percent of teens in grades 9-12 reported using synthetic growth hormone without a doctor's prescription. That number was a 6 percent jump from 2012.

In addition, the report said that African American and Hispanic teens are more likely than Caucasian teens to use HGH. Fifteen percent of African-American teens and 13 percent of Hispanic teens reported using HGH at least once in 2014, while 9 percent of Caucasian teens admitted to using the synthetic hormone. The survey concluded that 12 percent of teen boys and 9 percent of teen girls reported using HGH.

According to the Centers for Disease Control and Prevention (CDC), up to 11 percent of all high school males said they have tried steroids, despite

Teen athletes sometimes feel pressure to "bulk up" in order to be more competitive.

the health risks. Interestingly, 44 percent of high school seniors said they found it "very easy" or "fairly easy" to obtain the drugs. Such numbers are staggering, considering that in 2002 the University of Michigan reported only 4 percent of high school seniors and 3 percent of eight graders used steroids.

Why are teens so eager to take PEDs? Experts say there are many reasons. Some teens use the drugs because they have a negative image of their bodies. They hope that PEDs will make them stronger, more physically fit, or, as bodybuilders put it, more "cut." Still others use because their peers are using. They want to do what their friends are doing. They don't want to be excluded from the group.

Some teens take the drugs as a pattern of high-risk behaviors. Teens suffering from muscle **dysmorphia**, in which they see themselves as physically small and weak, may also misuse PEDs. Others take PEDS because they are under enormous pressure by parents, teammates, and coaches to succeed in sports. Athletic scholarships are at stake. In fact, doing well in sports may be the only way some high school athletes will ever attend college.

Teen athletes, especially males, are especially blinded by the perceived benefits of PEDs. Steroids promise bold results quickly. Most teens are blind to the negative effects of PEDs on physical and mental health.

Taylor Hooton was one teen who believed PEDs could help him skyrocket to the top. He was wrong. In 2002, Taylor, a pitcher for the Plano West Senior High School baseball team in Texas, longed to make the starting rotation. Fun-loving and popular, Taylor could throw strikes. In 2003, Taylor, then 17, killed himself. His parents, Don and Gwen Hooton, say their son's suicide was fueled by depression caused by Taylor's decision to stop using steroids.

Withdrawal from long-term steroid use is associated with a number of unpleasant physical and emotional symptoms. Perhaps of greatest concern, withdrawal can trigger depression—a condition characterized by feelings of sadness, hopelessness about the future, and decreased motivation.

PED ADDICTION

PEDs do not cause the same "high" as other drugs. Yet they can still be highly addictive. Research shows that rats will give themselves the drug whenever possible, a sure sign of addiction. Like other addictive drugs, PED use can affect a person's social relationships. People will also spend large amounts of money to get their hands on the drug. They can even experience withdrawal systems, such as mood swings, sleeplessness, and fatigue.

After their son's death, Don and Gwen Hooton started the Taylor Hooton Foundation to educate kids about the dangers of PEDs. Don Hooton testified before Congress in an attempt to pressure Major League Baseball to toughen its steroid policy. Hooton said major-league players are role models for many youngsters. These days, the foundation focuses on local school districts and has developed an online educational program for coaches and volunteers for Little League Baseball. It's been an uphill battle to get coaches and schools to get on board with the program. "For the moment," Don Hooton told a reporter in 2015, "we're the only ones fighting this battle."

TEXT-DEPENDENT QUESTIONS

1. How does EPO work?
2. What is blood doping?
3. What percentage of teens in grades 9-12 have reported using synthetic growth hormone without a doctor's prescription?

RESEARCH PROJECT

Use the library or the Internet to research the story of Taylor Hooton. Think about what other choices Taylor could have made that would have changed his situation. Create a list of alternative decisions Taylor could have made. Discuss your list with your classmates.

anemia: a blood condition in which there are too few red blood cells to carry oxygen, or there is a lack of hemoglobin.

DNA: short for deoxyribonucleic acid, a complex molecule that contains coded information needed for a cell to function.

endocrine system: the collection of glands that produce hormones to be carried throughout the body.

metabolism: the process by which food is turned into energy that the body uses to sustain life.

molecule: the smallest part of a chemical compound.

muscular hypertrophy: an increase in muscle mass.

neurotransmitter: a chemical in the body that moves messages between nerve cells.

ovaries: female reproductive organs that produce eggs and the sex hormones estrogen and progesterone.

puberty: the stage of physical development at which a person is capable of having children.

CHAPTER TWO

STEROIDS

Marion Jones always had Olympic gold on her mind. In 1984, when Jones was eight years old, she and her parents watched as runners carrying the Olympic torch ran past on their way to the Summer Olympics in Los Angeles. Later that night, Jones, alone in her room, took a piece of chalk and scribbled, "I want to be an Olympic champion" on a blackboard.

Jones's wish came true at the 2000 Summer Games in Sydney, Australia. Jones, a track-and-field star, won gold medals in the 100 meters, 200 meters, and the 4x400 meter relay. She also won two bronze medals, in the long jump and the 4x100 meter relay. No woman athlete had ever done so well. Jones was on the top of the world.

Seven years later, after the International Olympic Committee (IOC) began investigating allegations of her drug use, Jones admitted to using steroids before the 2000 Olympics. She said her coach, Trevor Graham, had given her a steroid nicknamed "the clear" beginning in 1999. The IOC stripped Jones of her medals. A judge later sentenced Jones to six months in prison for lying to federal agents about her PED use.

Marion Jones in 2006.

"The clear" is the nickname of an anabolic steroid called tetrahydrogestrinone, or THG. THG is a so-called designer steroid, cooked up by chemists in a laboratory and engineered not to be detected during drug tests. At the time, Jones and others used THG because of its stealth qualities. Many other athletes, including the NFL linebacker Bill Romanowski, Barry Bonds, and the U.S. sprinter Kelli White have all been implicated in using the clear. It is no longer undetectable, because tests can pinpoint the use of the substance.

For many athletes, anabolic-androgenic steroids are the PEDs of choice. They are chemicals synthesized from testosterone. *Anabolic* refers to muscle building. *Androgenic* refers to male characteristics such as facial hair and a deep voice.

LEGAL USES

Steroids were not invented to help athletes cheat, and the drugs do have legitimate medical value. In fact, doctors prescribe steroids every day for a variety of diseases and ailments. Steroids mimic testosterone, a hormone naturally created by the human body. In addition to helping males develop sexually, testosterone helps a person maintain healthy muscles and bones, and adequate levels of red blood cells. The cells provide oxygen to the body.

Testosterone, like other hormones, is a tiny chemical messenger. It moves through the bloodstream telling the body's cells and tissues what to do. Hormones are produced by the glands in the endocrine system. The endocrine system controls your mood, your growth, and your ability to have children. It also controls your metabolism, or the way your body converts food into energy. In men, testosterone is created in the testes, while women have small amounts of testosterone that is created in the ovaries.

Like most hormones, testosterone can only communicate with specific cells. When it finds those "target cells," muscles begin to grow. A protein molecule helps the receptors receive signals from testosterone. Because steroids are similar to testosterone, the receptors have no problem interacting with the drugs. Steroids set off a series of metabolic reactions, telling the body to increase the production of muscle tissue.

Doctors prescribe anabolic steroids to patients suffering from anemia, cancer, and HIV-AIDS. The drugs are also used to help some boys reach puberty. People with HIV-AIDS use steroids to build muscle mass. Doctors also prescribe the drugs to treat various inflammatory diseases, including rheumatoid arthritis.

NDC 0009-0417-02
10 ml Vial
Depo®-Testosterone
Sterile Solution
testosterone cypionate injection, USP
200 mg per ml
For intramuscular use only
Caution: Federal law prohibits dispensing without prescription.

Depo-Testosterone is a drug with legitimate medical uses, but it is often misused by people who have no real medical need for it.

MUSCLE BUILDING

People use anabolic steroids to speed up the to the body's ability to build muscle. Muscle fibers tear when a person exercises. The body naturally repairs those rips by adding larger cells to the fiber. It's a process is called **muscular hypertrophy**.

The more a person works out, the more muscle fiber he or she will rip. As a result, the body is constantly rebuilding muscle. As we said, steroids speed this process up. The drugs flow through the bloodstream until they are attracted to the receptor sites on the muscle. Those sites are called "androgen receptors." Steroids are offloaded onto the receptors and delivered to the cells of the muscle. Immediately, the drugs interact with the cell's **DNA**, stimulating the synthesis of protein. Proteins are the primary ingredients in muscle.

ON AND OFF

Most athletes who take anabolic steroids don't randomly inject themselves with the chemicals or pop pills as if they were eating candy. They are meticulous in their use, using a series of cycles. In this context, the term "cycle" refers to the specific number of weeks in which an athlete uses the drugs. "On-cycle" means they are on steroids. "Off-cycle" means they are not using steroids.

During each "on-cycle," athletes will often "stack," or take two or more types of anabolic steroids. The might inject some directly into their veins. Others they might take orally. Athletes stack to deliver the best possible results, depending on what goals they want to achieve. In most cases, testosterone is at the center of all stacking plans. However, there has been no scientific evidence to suggest that stacking works in the way the athletes hope.

STEROIDS AND THE LAW

Although the legal use of steroids varies around the world, in the United States steroids are illegal when used for nonmedical purposes. They are considered a "controlled substance," which means it is illegal to have them without a doctor's prescription. It is a federal crime, and a person can go to jail for a year. Selling steroids, or possessing them with intent to sell, is also a crime that can be punished with as many as 10 years in prison.

Steroids are also banned in professional sports. A few of the organizations that have banned steroid use include:

- Association of Tennis Professionals (ATP)
- International Federation of Association Football (FIFA)
- International Olympic Committee (IOC)
- Major League Baseball (MLB)
- National Basketball Association (NBA)
- National Hockey League (NHL)
- National Football League (NFL)
- World Wrestling Entertainment (WWE)

In 1999, the IOC created an organization called the World Anti-Doping Agency (WADA) to fight the use of performance-enhancing drugs in professional sports around the world. One of WADA's jobs is to monitor compliance with the World Anti-Doping Code, which came into effect in 2004. The code is regularly updated, and the most recent version of the document can be downloaded at WADA's website, https://www.wada-ama.org.

Athletes will also misuse steroids using a technique called "pyramiding." When an athlete is pyramiding, he or she will increase the amount and frequency of steroid use until they reach a certain level. In the first half of a 6- or 12-week cycle, the athlete will slowly increase the dose of each stacked drug. Around mid-cycle, they'll gradually taper their drug use back until they are not taking the drugs any longer. Some athletes will then train without drugs for a specific period.

Athletes believe pyramiding gives their bodies more time to adjust to the high doses of narcotics. Scientists have not tested whether cycling, stacking, or pyramiding provides any benefits.

ALL THE RAGE

All Rob Garibaldi wanted to do was win. He had all the makings of a major-league pitcher, except one. He was too small. He had to bulk up, get bigger, and then he might be able to pitch in the big leagues. His coach told him to put on weight. The guy who sold him legal weight-gaining substances told Rob the same thing. Even the trainers at the University of Southern California told Garibaldi he needed to get bigger. With visions of major-league success dancing through his head, Garibaldi decided to take a shortcut: steroids. His psychiatrist, Dr. Brent Cox, said Garibaldi used so many steroids over the years that he had numerous violent outbursts. Cox told the *San Francisco Chronicle*, "There was a really edgy, irritable quality when he was using steroids, like he was just ready to jump across the room and throttle you." When Garibaldi off-cycled, he would sink into a long depression.

The rage incidents ended when Garibaldi killed himself at the age of 24. The story highlights one of the most dramatic side effects of steroid use, which has come to be known as "roid rage." Although various scientific studies show conflicting results on whether there is a link between

Jose Canseco bats for the Yuma Scorpions in 2011. Canseco has said that when he played in Major League Baseball in the late 1980s and 1990s, about 80 percent of the players were "doping."

WHAT'S IN A NAME?

Steroids go by many names, including "juice," "roids," "hype," and "pump." They are also called "Arnolds," after one of the greatest bodybuilders of all time. Long before Arnold Schwarzenegger was a movie star and the governor of California, he was a ripped body builder, the most famous in the world. He won the Mr. Olympia competition seven times, Mr. Universe five times, and was a one-time Mr. World champion.

Schwarzenegger's success led to countless magazine covers, starring roles in Hollywood blockbusters, and finally his election as governor of California. Still, as he readily admits, steroids were the foundation of all his achievements. He told an interviewer that using steroids was "stupid," but "not illegal as it is now." He said he used steroids during the 1960s and 1970s, "when we didn't know any better." He went on to say, "we want to keep the sport clean. It says 'bodybuilding,' not 'body destroying.'"

A monument to Arnold-as-bodybuilder, in the Arnold Schwarzenegger Museum in his hometown of Thal, Austria.

steroid use and aggressive behavior in humans, other studies show a clear relationship between testosterone and aggression.

One study, conducted in 2006, clearly showed a link between rage and steroids in hamsters. Researchers began their experiment by giving tame hamsters anabolic steroids. Soon after, the critters became highly aggressive. When scientists stopped giving the rodents the juice, 85 percent remained violent. Researchers then conducted autopsies on the hamsters. They found that animals' brains had changed. They said the hypothalamus, the part of the brain that controls involuntary functions such as body temperature and the release of hormones, created excess vasopressin, a neurotransmitter associated with aggressive behavior.

As one researcher said, the steroids stepped "on the gas for aggression" by stimulating the areas of the brain that affect anger. "Some of the effects may wear off after withdrawal, but aggressive behavior won't stop immediately, leaving them to be a danger to themselves and others," said the study's leader, Richard Melloni Jr.

PHYSICAL SIDE EFFECTS

Acne. Breast development in men. Heart attacks. Liver cancer. Hair loss in women. The list of side effects from steroid use seems endless. Scientists are now beginning to understand the long-term effects of steroids on the body. Although the drugs have been around for a while, it is difficult to get users to agree to be part of any study, and this may have slowed down efforts to research the effects of the drugs. Nevertheless, scientists have determined that steroids can wreak havoc on many bodily functions. For one thing, steroids affect the body's normal production of hormones, which can cause many problems for men, including reduced sperm count due to the shrinking of the testes. Many men will go bald. Some will even develop breasts. Acne is common.

ADDICTION AND STEROIDS

Even though media stories about steroid use focuses on athletes, professional athletes make up a small fraction of steroid users. Most adult men who use steroids are not professional athletes, but average guys. According to Harvard researchers, about 3 million American men have used steroids at some point in their lives. About a third are dependent on the drugs and have taken them for years.

Are you addicted to steroids? You might be and not know it. Like any other addictive drug, you can start to believe you need PEDs. Cutting back is hard. Moreover, you find yourself spending more time and money using them, even though you know they are bad for you. These are all signs of possible addiction.

Celebrity athletes might get all the attention, but most of the people misusing steroids are regular folks.

In women, steroid use can cause a woman's voice to deepen. Women can also find themselves growing facial hair, but losing the hair on their heads. Their skin can turn from smooth to rough. For adolescent children, excessive steroid use can trick the body into thinking the child's bones have stopped growing. This can lead to permanent stunting of height and prevent teens from getting taller.

Steroids also increase the risk of blood clots, which can disrupt the flow of blood through a person's body. Because the clots affect the heart's ability to pump blood efficiently, damage can occur to the heart muscles, resulting in a heart attack. Steroids can also cause liver damage and internal bleeding.

MORE SIDE EFFECTS

Steroid use can impact the body in many ways. The following is a list of common physical side effects for both males and females.

Males and Females	Females	Males
• hair loss	• facial hair growth	• testicular shrinkage
• dizziness	• development of deep voice	• painful urination
• mood swings	• shrinking of the breasts	• breast development
• sleep problems	• changes in menstruation	• inability to get an erection
• nausea		
• shaking		
• high blood pressure		
• joint pain		

Source: Council on Drug Abuse, "What Are Performance-Enhancing Drugs and How Can We Prevent Our Youth from Using?" http://www.drugabuse.ca/what-are-performance-enhancing-drugs-and-how-can-we-prevent-our-youth-using.

BRAIN DRAIN

Steroids can also harm the brain, as a recent study reported. Beginning in the fall of 2013 and running through the summer of 2014, researchers at McLean Hospital, which is affiliated with Harvard Medical School, looked at the brain scans of 150 male weightlifters that had been using steroids for a long time. Scientists then compared those images to the brain scans of those not on the drugs. It was the first major study of its kind.

What scientists found was alarming. Inside the brain is a region called the amygdala, the brain's emotional center. The amygdala is the part of the brain responsible for how we respond to fear, and it also plays a role in depression, anxiety, and aggression. Researchers found that the amygdala in those abusing steroids was 20 percent larger than in those who had never taken the drugs. "That is a really marked difference," said Dr. Marc J. Kaufman, who helped conduct the study. "It is particularly interesting

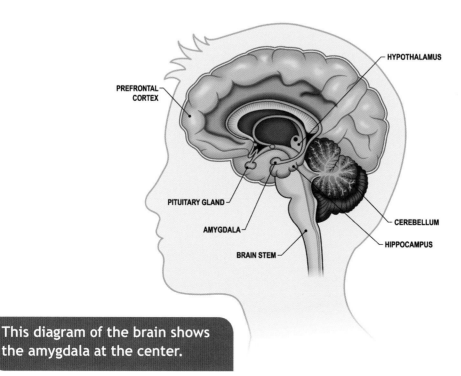

This diagram of the brain shows the amygdala at the center.

because previous studies have shown that amygdala enlargement has been associated with aggression among other types of substance abuse populations."

Another discovery showed a decrease in the level of a particular brain sugar. The lack of the sugar plays a role in the development of Alzheimer's disease, which causes problems with memory, thinking, and behavior.

The major problem, researchers say, is that steroids stay in a person's system longer than alcohol and most other drugs. For instance, while cocaine leaves a person's system within a few hours, steroids can keep a person's testosterone levels 20 to 40 times higher than normal for several days. Combine this with the fact that weightlifters cycle and continuously use steroids over a specific period of time, and the body does not get a rest from the drugs. They are stored in body fat, where they remain for weeks.

TEXT-DEPENDENT QUESTIONS

1. What hormone do anabolic steroids mimic?
2. Explain "cycling" as it relates to steroid use.
3. Name three legitimate medical uses of steroids.

RESEARCH PROJECT

Create an advertising message about the dangers of steroid use. Use whatever medium you want. For example, your advertisement can be in the form of a video, a computer slide presentation, an audio presentation, or a poster.

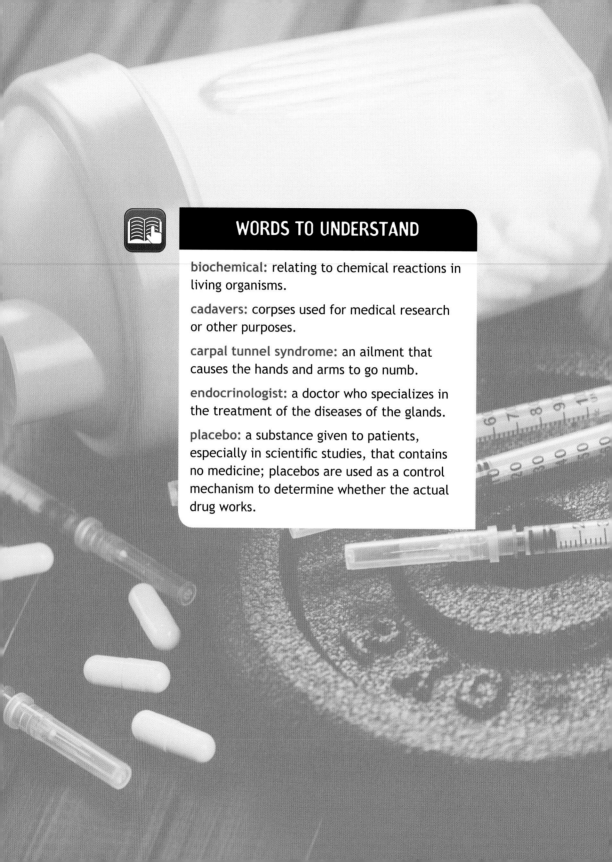

WORDS TO UNDERSTAND

biochemical: relating to chemical reactions in living organisms.

cadavers: corpses used for medical research or other purposes.

carpal tunnel syndrome: an ailment that causes the hands and arms to go numb.

endocrinologist: a doctor who specializes in the treatment of the diseases of the glands.

placebo: a substance given to patients, especially in scientific studies, that contains no medicine; placebos are used as a control mechanism to determine whether the actual drug works.

CHAPTER THREE

HGH AND OTHER HORMONES

Elliott Hulse is a beefy guy. His arms are ripped. His stomach is like a washboard. His biceps are cut and sculpted. His neck is thick. His chest is hard as rock. The picture on his website shows what appears to be a determined athlete, a bodybuilder who blogs and creates videos for like-minded athletes. The site's trademarked tagline beckons would-be muscle heads to become the "Strongest Version of Themselves."

It seems that Hulse loves to work out. If you dig deeper, you'll find a YouTube video explaining a bit how he got so big. Titled "Should I Use HGH?" Hulse, a self-described former steroid user, says human growth hormone (HGH) is a wonder drug.

"Yes, it does work," he says in the video. "I have friends who are competing in Strongman and other sports . . . they look good and they are strong. They are basically using this synthetic hormone. Do I think you should use it or not? Use it—just remain objective the entire time. Don't

Many teens get their performance-enhancing drugs online.

lean on it so heavily that it becomes an integral part of who you are. Because it's not."

Scientists and others would tell you not to listen to Hulse and others who extol the perceived virtues of HGH. It can slowly wreck your body. Many don't even know what they are using. Yet teens don't seem to be getting the message.

As the Partnership for Drug-Free Kids survey underscores, teens are using HGH in record numbers. Eleven percent of teens in grades 9 through 12 say they have used HGH with a doctor's prescription. In addition, 22 percent of teens say they are well aware of how companies market steroids and synthetic HGH on the Internet. Moreover, teens are less likely to believe that using PEDs is a risky behavior. The study also found that teens are using these substances in an attempt not only to improve their on-field abilities, but also to bolster other parts of their lives, such as how they look.

GROWTH SPURT

Human growth hormone does just what it name suggests. Produced naturally by a pea-sized organ called the pituitary gland found at the base of the brain, HGH fuels growth and development in children. It also helps regulate various body systems, including cardiac functions and the metabolism of sugar and fat. The levels of HGH peak during the teen years and decline as people get older.

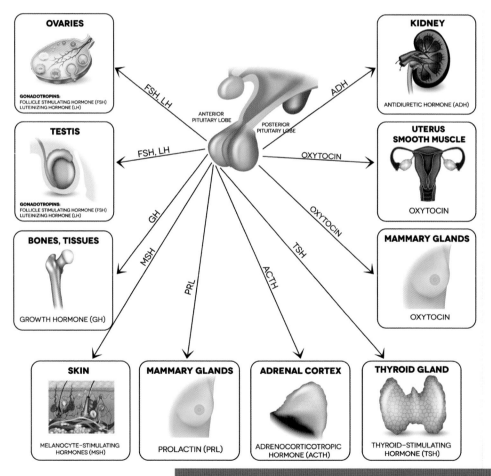

A tiny gland at the base of the brain, the pituitary affects a huge number of bodily systems.

TESTOSTERONE VERSUS HGH

Although testosterone and HGH are important for muscle growth, there is one notable difference between the two. Testosterone is a single molecule, while HGH is a string of 191 molecules known as amino acids. Amino acids make proteins that cells desperately need to function. The molecules of amino acids are long and large, resembling a string of pearls. Each of those pearls is an amino acid that can band together to make thousands of different proteins. HGH needs to be injected to do the most good. That's because acid in the stomach breaks down each amino acid if a person takes HGH orally or through inhalers.

First isolated by scientists in 1956, researchers did not map HGH's biochemical structure until the early 1970s. By the 1960s, however, it became clear that underdeveloped children could benefit by HGH therapy. HGH works because it stimulates the liver, allowing the organ to make a protein that spurs bone and muscle growth.

At the time there was only way to get HGH—from cadavers. For more than 20 years, that was the only way HGH could be extracted. The method came to a crashing halt in 1985, when it was discovered that some HGH was contaminated with a deadly disease, similar to mad cow disease. Twenty-six people died because of the tainted hormone, and the U.S. Food and Drug Administration put an immediate end to cadaver HGH.

But by that time, scientists had found a way to make synthetic HGH by using genetically modified bacteria. The scientists manipulated the DNA of the tiny organisms, turning them into HGH pumping stations. It was a significant breakthrough. Thousands of children immediately benefitted from the synthetic version of HGH, including Cutler Dozier, who at the age of 14 weighed only 76 pounds and was smaller than a typical 12-year-old.

Cutler was growing no more than one-half inches a year, significantly less than the yearly average of two inches. Although the boy's doctor was not concerned, Cutler's mother was. She took her son to see a pediatric endocrinologist, a doctor who specializes in treating disorders of the endocrine system. The doctor said the boy's body was not producing enough HGH. He recommended Cutler undergo treatment. Cutler is now a normal adult who stands nearly six-feet tall.

THE EFFECTIVENESS OF HGH

The discovery of synthetic HGH was a boon for athletes. They believed that if they took high doses of HGH they would have more energy and bigger muscles. As a result, they believed they would perform better on the field. Athletes also used HGH to recover from injuries faster. Unlike anabolic steroids, HGH didn't make a person aggressive, although it did have other side effects, such as joint pain and low blood sugar. Athletes also loved HGH

Whether HGH will really improve athletic performance remains uncertain; the risks, on the other hand, are not.

because it could not be detected by a test. (That has since changed, and many sports now test for HGH use.)

But does HGH work? Or have users risked their health and reputations on something that doesn't work? It's possible. An often-cited Stanford University study published in 2008 found that the drug might not improve athletic performance in the way some might think. The study found that HGH increased the amount of lean muscle mass by forcing the body to retain fluids. However, it did not make anyone stronger. In fact, the study concluded that HGH might cause athletes to become more tired. The study looked at the results of 44 previous studies and found that people who took HGH gained about 4.6 pounds. However, not all that weight translated into strength. In fact, those who took HGH were more like to get injured. They developed joint pain and carpal tunnel syndrome.

However, some scientists caution that such studies might not be accurate. There were limits on the studies. The doses of HGH used by those participating in the research were not very high. Moreover, test subjects took HGH only for a brief period, whereas athletes who use HGH as part of their workout routine take high doses for years.

HGH SIDE EFFECTS

Like all PEDs, HGH use can lead to major side effects. They include diabetes along with the abnormal growth of bones and organs. HGH use can also lead to high blood pressure and hardening of the arteries, a condition called atherosclerosis. Leukemia, a cancer of the blood, has also been reported in a few users. The more common side effects include blurred vision, numbness, dizziness, constant ear infections, severe headaches, and nervousness. Like other PEDS, a person can become dependent on HGH. They can have problems stopping or cutting back use.

Another study, this one conducted in 2010, concluded that athletes do benefit from HGH use. Researchers at the Garvan Institute of Medical Research in Australia tested 103 males and females, aged 18 to 40. All were recreational athletes. Researchers split the men and women into two groups. One group received HGH injections. The others received salt water injections. All of the athletes then rode exercise bikes, lifted weights, and performed jump tests.

After two months, those taking HGH did not become stronger or have more endurance than those who took the placebo. However, their speed on the exercise bike increased by 4 percent, while the speed of males who were given HGH and testosterone improved by 8 percent. Once again, the test subjects did not receive as much HGH as professional athletes who misuse the drugs.

"We used lower doses of growth hormone than athletes are reported to use, and for a shorter time," said Professor Ken Ho, head of pituitary research at Garvan. "We can speculate, therefore, that the drug's effects on performance might be greater than shown in this study." However, Garvan also noted that "its side effects might be more serious [than we thought]."

ABUSING EPO

For years, Lance Armstrong denied using PEDs, including a hormone called EPO, short for erythropoietin, a human growth hormone that jumpstarts the production of red blood cells. Tyler Hamilton, part of Armstrong's U.S. cycling team, took Armstrong to task for his denials. He said the two of them, along with other members of the team, used PEDs on a regular basis, including EPO, a powerful PED. For endurance cyclists who dope, EPO is the Holy Grail of performance-enhancing drugs. The hormone, which is produced in the kidneys, increases the number of oxygen-carrying red blood cells. Hamilton says EPO boosted his performance about 5 percent,

Tyler Hamilton in 2009. Hamilton has criticized fellow cyclist Lance Armstrong for his dishonesty about their EPO use.

"roughly the difference between first place in the Tour de France and the middle of the pack."

EPO works fast, but a test can detect the hormone in the body for several hours after an athlete takes is. Hamilton said Armstrong and other members of the U.S. team kept scrupulous track of when they used the drug. They even let each other know when the drug tester came around. Of course, Hamilton, Armstrong, and the other members of the U.S. team weren't the only cyclists doping with EPO. More than half the Tour de France winners since 1980 were dopers.

HOW DOES IT WORK?

EPO first made its way onto the sports scene in the 1980s. The drug, which like HGH and testosterone, can be made in a laboratory, makes it easier for the body to deliver oxygen from the lungs to the muscles.

There are special sensors in the kidneys that measure the flow of oxygen in the blood. If the amount of oxygen drops below a certain level, the kidneys start producing EPO, which is released into the bloodstream. Special receptors on bone marrow wait for the hormone to arrive. When it does, they grab hold and never let go. EPO excites the cells in the bone marrow, spurring the creation of more red blood cells, which means there's more oxygen that muscles can use.

Synthetic EPO, also known by the brand name Epogen, works the same way. Epogen was created to help people suffering from anemia, but it has been used for many years by athletes. Athletes who can ramp up the number of red blood cells in their bodies are able to produce oxygen for a longer period. Oxygen helps muscles work more effectively, creating an increase in performance and giving doped-up athletes an unfair advantage over those that don't use the substance.

EPO side effects range from an uptick in blood pressure to seizures. Those who misuse the drug might experience headaches, joint pain, trouble sleeping, and vomiting. It can also cause your heart to work harder, leading to coronary problems such as a stroke. Like other PEDs, the body begins to crave EPO, and stopping use can be difficult.

TEXT-DEPENDENT QUESTIONS

1. Which part of the body naturally produces human growth hormone?
2. How is synthetic HGH made in the laboratory?
3. Explain how EPO increases the amount of oxygen flowing to the muscles.

RESEARCH PROJECT

Find out more about athletes who have admitted taking HGH or EPO, and the effect those drugs had on them. Create a chart showing how HGH or EPO impacted their professional and personal lives. You can find this information by searching specific athletes and "HGH use" on the Internet.

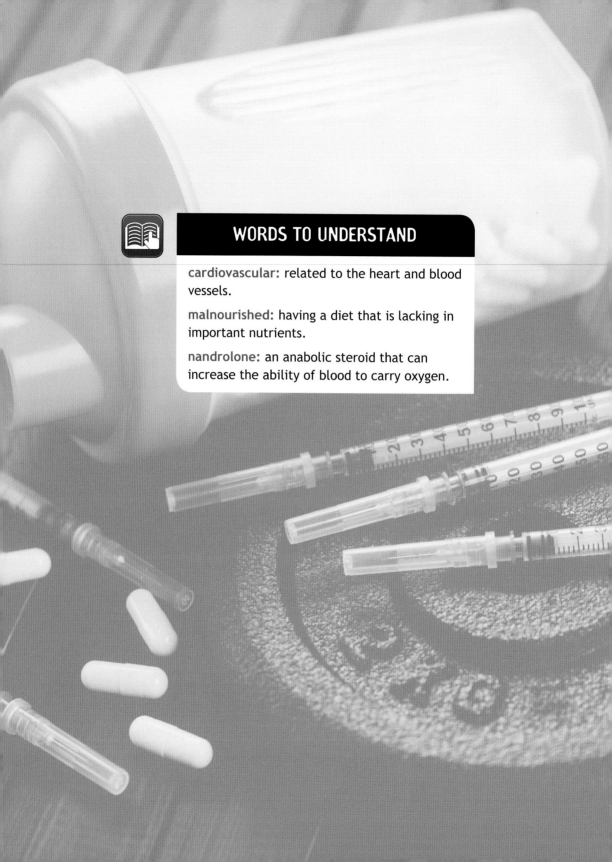

WORDS TO UNDERSTAND

cardiovascular: related to the heart and blood vessels.

malnourished: having a diet that is lacking in important nutrients.

nandrolone: an anabolic steroid that can increase the ability of blood to carry oxygen.

CHAPTER FOUR

SPORTS SUPPLEMENTS

It was baseball spring training 2003, and Kellie Bechler was seven months pregnant as she drove from Oregon to Florida to be with her husband, Steve. Both were in their early 20s. Steve, who had been a standout pitcher on the South Medford High School baseball team in Oregon, was in South Florida hoping to pitch for the Baltimore Orioles, a Major League baseball team.

On February 16, under the hot Fort Lauderdale sun, Steve Bechler complained of feeling dizzy. He turned pale and then collapsed. An ambulance whisked Bechler to the hospital. Kellie heard the news while on the road. She ditched her car and took the first plane to Florida. She was with her husband when he died 24 hours later. The medical examiner ruled the death was caused, in part, by a performance-enhancing supplement called ephedra.

Unlike anabolic steroids or HGH, which are made in labs, ephedra is made from a plant called *Ephedra sinica,* which is native to Central Asia

Steve Belcher died while using ephedra to boost his chances of getting picked by the Baltimore Orioles.

and Mongolia. The main ingredient is ephedrine, a chemical compound that overstimulates a person's nervous and cardiovascular systems. It imitates the natural effects of adrenaline, which a person's body releases when he or she is excited, angry, or fearful. Adrenaline gives a person more energy and causes the heart to beat faster. Although there is minimal proven benefit to taking ephedra, people used the supplement believing it would help them lose weight, gain energy, and enhance their performance on the field.

Ephedra had already proved deadly before Bechler's case. Between 1995 and 1997, more than 900 complaints about ephedra flooded into the offices of the U.S. Food and Drug Administration. During that period, 37 cases of sudden death were reported.

Kellie Bechler and several others took the manufacturer of the supplement to court. The company argued Steve Bechler did not follow the instructions on the label. The case was eventually settled, and the terms of the agreement were never released. Bechler's death, however, was a wake-up call to the dangers of natural dietary and performance-enhancing supplements. The pitcher's death spurred the government to ban ephedrine in dietary supplements. It is a highly addictive drug; signs of addiction may include restlessness, irritability, and memory loss.

ON THE MARKET

"The Clear Pill That Builds Muscle."

"Extreme muscle builder supplement that helps you build lean muscles fast and effective."

"Supercharge Your Workout."

The advertisements are bold. You see them in magazines, accompanied by puffed up weightlifters and women in bikinis with washboard abs. They are on the Internet, and on television. They stare at you from the counters of drug stores and health food stores. They promise more energy, more muscle, and more strength. Athletes, such as the major league pitcher Clayton Kershaw, lifestyle coach Kathleen Tesori, professional trainer and TV celebrity Jillian Michaels, and Olympic marathoner Ryan Hall, have all touted their use.

Performance-enhancing supplements come in many varieties. You can get them just about anywhere: drug stores, health food stores, and on the Internet. Some are pills. Others are powders or liquids. They contain many ingredients. Most claim to boost athletic performance by increasing muscle mass and recovery time

Ephedra is commonly used in Chinese medicine—but that doesn't mean that it's safe to use on your own.

between workouts. Some are vitamins or minerals. Others are herbs. Still others are amino acids.

While doctors sometimes recommend these supplements to patients who are **malnourished** or who might have special dietary needs, athletes and individuals trying to get stronger take them by the spoonful believing they are a safe way to increase on-field performance. Yet most don't know what they are taking, and the list of ingredients might not tell the entire story. The health consequences can be damaging.

Such sports supplements are considered dietary, or nutritional, supplements. The FDA regulates them as food, not as drugs. The only time the FDA can take action is when a supplement has been found unsafe after it is already on the store shelves. Unlike prescription drugs, which are subject to years of scientific review—including testing and scrutiny by prominent researchers—sports supplements do not undergo rigorous scientific examination. The nutritional supplement business is one of the fastest-growing industries in the world, producing about $32 billion in revenue in 2012. That number is expected to top $60 billion by 2021. Studies show that novice and professional athletes are the top users of dietary or performance-enhancing supplements.

BUYER BEWARE

What an athlete sees on the label of a sports supplement is often not what they get. The International Olympic Committee's anti-doping lab found that of the 634 supplements it tested, 14.8 percent contained testosterone and **nandrolone**, an anabolic steroid, which were never listed as ingredients.

Researchers have also found other dangerous ingredients. One, DMAA, contributed to the death of 30-year-old Claire Squires, who died while participating in the London Marathon in 2012. Doctors found "signifiant levels" of DMAA in her blood. DMAA is a substance that elevates a person's

Crowds of runners in the 2012 London Marathon.

TEENS AND SUPPLEMENTS

In December 2012 the journal *Pediatrics* reported that 25 percent of adolescent boys have used muscle-building supplements at least once. Many of the 3,000 teens surveyed in the report were not involved in team sports. The study also confirmed what most scientists already knew: some supplements contain ingredients that can have serious adverse health consequences or cause death.

"Many of these substances are essentially hormones, so the side effects are related to changes in secondary sex characteristics—facial hair growth in women, breast development in men," said Maria Eisenberg, from the University of Minnesota. "This could have lasting effects for young people going through puberty."

A 2006 study of teenagers in one upstate New York county found that more than 25 percent used herbal supplements. Moreover, the study underscored the risks teens take in becoming addicted to supplements. Researchers say it is a gateway to abusing other drugs. Compared with teens who have never used the herbal products, those that did were nearly 5 times more likely to have used LSD, PCP, and ecstasy, among other drugs. They were 6 times more likely to have tried cocaine, and nearly 15 times more likely to have used steroids.

blood pressure and can ultimately lead to cardiac arrest. Like ephedra in the Steve Bechler death, DMAA was not illegal when Squires used it.

Squires collapsed just a mile from the finish line. Her boyfriend told authorities that she might have ingested the banned substance after drinking a supplement she bought on the Internet. DMAA is now illegal in Great Britain as well as the United States.

CREATINE

Creatine is one of the more popular supplements used by professional and teen athletes. A 2001 study in the journal *Pediatrics* reported that 44 percent of high school senior boys in Westchester County, New York, said they had taken creatine.

Creatine is natural substance found in food such as meat and fish. The body also makes some creatine. Once creatine is in the body, it changes to a compound called phosphocreatine. Creatine helps the body generate more energy by repairing a molecule in a compound called ATP, or adenosine triphosphate. ATP provides muscles with energy. Creatine restores the broken-down ATP molecule, allowing the body to quickly generate more energy. Supplements increase the pool of creatine that can power ATP.

Athletes use the supplement in their workout routines to increase muscle mass and improve strength. They also use it to help their muscles recover more quickly after exercise. Some studies suggest 8 percent of adolescents take creatine, as do 40 percent of college athletes. Nearly half of professional athletes say they take the supplement. Whether

WHO USES CREATINE?

Do you know anyone who takes creatine? You might. According to the *Encyclopedia of Adolescence*, creatine use among teen athletes fluctuates between sports and genders. Here's a breakdown:

Girls	Boys
track and field: 5.4 percent	football: 30.1 percent
gymnastics: 4.7 percent	swimming: 28.4 percent
tennis: 4.6 percent	hockey: 28 percent
volleyball: 3.8 percent	baseball: 26.5 percent

Venison (deer meat) and other wild game are the best natural sources of creatine. Other lean red meats and some fish (salmon, herring, and tuna) are also good sources.

the promises of creatine are actual or exaggerated is still up in the air. Some studies claim creatine works as advertised, giving athletes better performance during short bursts of athletic activity. Other studies say creatine does not work for endurance athletes.

DANGERS OF SPORTS SUPPLEMENTS

In 2015, researchers published a study that underscored the link between some sports supplements and cancer. They discovered that men who took muscle-building powders and pills containing creatine or the hormone androstenedione have a higher risk of testicular cancer. The risk was extremely high for anyone who used the supplements before they turned 25, used multiple supplements, or who used the supplements for many years.

Researchers found that those who used bodybuilding supplements had a 65 percent greater risk of developing testicular cancer, compared to those who did not use the supplements. The odds increased for those who used more than one supplement.

TEXT-DEPENDENT QUESTIONS

1. What are the differences between performance-enhancing drugs and performance-enhancing supplements?
2. In which foods is creatine found?
3. According to the journal *Pediatrics*, what percentage of male teens have used body-building supplements at least once?

RESEARCH PROJECT

Find an advertisement for a performance-enhancing supplement. You can find them on the Internet or in magazines. Evaluate the ad based on these criteria:

- What is the target audience of this ad?
- What claims does this ad make but not state outright?
- What claims does it *suggest*?
- Does the ad provide any evidence to back up its claims?
- If so, what is that "evidence"?
- Are there any warnings on the label?

Once you have evaluated the ad, do you trust it? Are the claims in the ad truthful? Why or why not? Would you use this product? Why or why not?

FURTHER READING

BOOKS AND ARTICLES

Henningfield, Jack E. *Steroids: Pumped Up and Dangerous.* Illicit and Misused Drugs. Broomall, PA: Mason Crest, 2014.

Lau, Doretta. *Steroids.* Incredibly Disgusting Drugs. New York: Rosen Publishing Group, 2008.

LeVert, Suzanne. *The Facts about Steroids.* Tarrytown, NY: Benchmark Books, 2005.

Scott, Celicia. *Doping: Human Growth Hormone, Steroids and Other Performance-Enhancing Drugs.* Broomall, PA: Mason Crest, 2015.

Sommers, Annie Leah. *College Athletics: Steroids and Supplement Abuse.* New York: Rosen Publishing Group, 2010.

ONLINE

Kids Health. "Are Steroids Worth the Risk?" http://kidshealth.org/teen/food_fitness/sports/steroids.html.

National Institute of Drug Abuse. "Drug Facts: Anabolic Steroids." http://teens.drugabuse.gov/drug-facts/anabolic-steroids.

Play Healthy. Partnership for Drug-Free Kids. http://playhealthy.drugfree.org/.

Taylor Hooton Foundation. http://taylorhooton.org/.

U.S. Food and Drug Administration. "Teens and Steroids: A Dangerous Combo." http://www.fda.gov/ForConsumers/ConsumerUpdates/ucm373014.htm.

EDUCATIONAL VIDEOS

Access these videos with your smartphone or use the URLs below to find them online.

"Doping Scandals Throughout History," CNN. "CNN's Andy Scholes recounts some of the world's most notorious sports doping scandals." https://youtu.be/4l_1sWxEt8U

"Peformance-Enhancing Drugs," SciShow (a YouTube channel dedicated to scientific information). "You've heard about them, but do you know how they work? Or why they suck? Hank [of SciShow] explains the science behind performance enhancers." https://youtu.be/qfxoqje1X7o

"Anabolic Steroids." National Geographic Documentaries. "Anabolic steroids are drugs that are structurally related to the cyclic steroid ring systems and have similar effects to testosterone in the body." https://youtu.be/DDlZJdTbHHA

"Pure Performance," Australian Sports Antidoping Authority (ASADA). "Dr David Hughes talks about nutrition and supplements in sport," https://youtu.be/WTN7JX93RsQ

"10 Worst Side Effects of Steroid Abuse," TheRichest (a YouTube channel dedicated to sharing surprising and often controversial information). "Top 10 worst things that can happen to bodybuilders when they overuse steroids." https://youtu.be/Hxq6xCa8Dm8

SERIES GLOSSARY

abstention: actively choosing to not do something.

acute: something that is intense but lasts a short time.

alienation: a sense of isolation or detachment from a larger group.

alleviate: to lessen or relieve.

binge: doing something to excess.

carcinogenic: something that causes cancer.

chronic: ongoing or recurring.

cognitive: having to do with thought.

compulsion: a desire that is very hard or even impossible to resist.

controlled substance: a drug that is regulated by the government.

coping mechanism: a behavior a person learns or develops in order to manage stress.

craving: a very strong desire for something.

decriminalized: something that is not technically legal but is no longer subject to prosecution.

depressant: a substance that slows particular bodily functions.

detoxify: to remove toxic substances (such as drugs or alcohol) from the body.

ecosystem: a community of living things interacting with their environment.

environment: one's physical, cultural, and social surroundings.

genes: units of inheritance that are passed from parent to child and contain information about specific traits and characteristics.

hallucinate: seeing things that aren't there.

hyperconscious: to be intensely aware of something.

illicit: illegal; forbidden by law or cultural custom.

inhibit: to limit or hold back.

interfamilial: between and among members of a family.

metabolize: the ability of a living organism to chemically change compounds.

neurotransmitter: a chemical substance in the brain.

paraphernalia: the equipment used for producing or ingesting drugs, such as pipes or syringes.

physiological: relating to the way an organism functions.

placebo: a medication that has no physical effect and is used to test whether new drugs actually work.

predisposition: to be more inclined or likely to do something.

prohibition: when something is forbidden by law.

recidivism: a falling back into past behaviors, especially criminal ones.

recreation: something done for fun or enjoyment.

risk factors: behaviors, traits, or influences that make a person vulnerable to something.

sobriety: the state of refraining from alcohol or drugs.

social learning: a way that people learn behaviors by watching other people.

stimulant: a class of drug that speeds up bodily functions.

stressor: any event, thought, experience, or biological or chemical function that causes a person to feel stress.

synthetic: made by people, often to replicate something that occurs in nature.

tolerance: the state of needing more of a particular substance to achieve the same effect.

traffic: to illegally transport people, drugs, or weapons to sell throughout the world.

withdrawal: the physical and psychological effects that occur when a person with a use disorder suddenly stops using substances.

INDEX

ABOUT THE AUTHOR

John Perritano is an award-winning journalist, writer, and editor from Southbury CT., who has written numerous articles and books on a variety of subjects including science, sports, history, and culture for such publishers as Mason Crest, National Geographic, Scholastic and Time/Life. His articles have appeared on Discovery.com, Popular Mechanics.com and other magazines and Web sites. He holds a Master's Degree in American History from Western Connecticut State University.

ABOUT THE ADVISOR

Sara Becker, Ph.D. is a clinical researcher and licensed clinical psychologist specializing in the treatment of adolescents with substance use disorders. She is an Assistant Professor (Research) in the Center for Alcohol and Addictions Studies at the Brown School of Public Health and the Evaluation Director of the New England Addiction Technology Transfer Center. Dr. Becker received her Ph.D. in Clinical Psychology from Duke University and completed her clinical residency at Harvard Medical School's McLean Hospital. She joined the Center for Alcohol and Addictions Studies as a postdoctoral fellow and transitioned to the faculty in 2011. Dr. Becker directs a program of research funded by the National Institute on Drug Abuse that explores novel ways to improve the treatment of adolescents with substance use disorders. She has authored over 30 peer-reviewed publications and book chapters and serves on the Editorial Board of the *Journal of Substance Abuse Treatment*.

PHOTO CREDITS

Photos are for illustrative purposes only; individuals depicted are models.
Cover Photo: Shutterstock/Nickola_Che
Drug Enforcement Agency: 27
iStock.com: 7 PeopleImages; 15 PeopleImages; 16 Renphoto; 18 hidesy; 34 BraunS; 36 James Kopp; 40 monkeybusinessimages
Shutterstock: 12 Marc Pagani Photography; 17 Serghei Starus; 21 Nagel Photography; 32 posztos; 41 Tefi; 43 FCG; 51 Maryilyn Barbone; 53 Michael Puche; 56 Stine Lise Nielsen
Wikimedia Commons: 26 Thomas Faivre-Duboz; 31 Resolute; 46 Christina; 50 Keith Allison